The jumper

"Hello, Lucy, what are you making?"

"I'm making a jumper," said Lucy.

"Is it for you?"

16

"No, it's not too big," said Fred.

"Oh . . . . . .
It's too big!" said Lucy.

"Here you are, Barney."

13

"It's for Barney."

"Yes, it is," said Lucy.

"Is it for Barney?"

"No, it's not," said Lucy.

"Is it for me?"

"No, it's not," said Lucy.

"Is it for me?"

"No, it's not," said Lucy.